HAPPY HOUSE

Simple Steps on How You Can Make Big Money Owning and Operating Your own Housekeeping Business with $300.00 or Less

---

BARBARA NETHERY

Acknowledgment

All content in this book is genuine and are my own experiences.

A collection of twenty-five years' experience as owner and operator of Happy House Detail Cleaning in Panama City Beach, Florida

Preface

Simple and Easy Instructions.

It was 1979 in Anaheim, California; I had applied for a housekeeping position at one of the high rise hotels that I had found in the local paper. While completing the application, I could not believe all those questions they ask; my thought was I am a girl; every girl knows how to clean a house.

I didn't get the job. I was amazed. Why didn't they pick me? What I know today is that all people know how to clean to please themselves, but cleaning to please other people is another thing. Years later, in 1981, I moved to Panama City Beach, FL. A tourist town filled with all types of cleaning needs.

I then applied again for a cleaning job. This time I was hired. The business was operated by a wonderful lady named Monique. She was from France, and boy was she a cleaning freak, so I thought. And she would always ask, did you do this or that? And she went to check no matter what the answer was.

I worked and learned from Ms. Monique for about two years. I then decided I would try my luck at residential homes and construction cleaning. I soon realized we have two different mindsets here. I was fortunate to find a teacher who was a lady who had been cleaning many years, and she taught me a lot. After stepping out on my own, it took me about three years to build a full-time schedule. I made a lot of mistakes along the way, but proud to say twenty-three years later, still going strong. I love this profession mainly because you get to meet so many people and serve them, many times in an area they are physically disabled.

You can pick your hours and make good money. I have laid out a plan to succeed, and I hope you will grab hold and enjoy the ride.

Happy Cleaning

Contents

ONE

What is a Housekeeper?

Remember the Carol Burnett photo that was so popular? The lady with the mop and her foot in the bucket? And the maids in the movie The Color Purple and, of course, the movie Maids. These images could portray a poor, uneducated, overworked woman that is barely getting by — these are not the pictures of a professional housekeeper of today.

We are not maids; we are professional housekeepers. There is a big difference.

Let us first look at the maid and her duties.

Maid

This position is much needed and should be viewed with respect and honor. Useful for various reasons, they are not only a maid, but they also serve as housekeepers; they are also fulfilling a servant's position to the clients. Their primary focus is to keep the Client happy and care for their needs and their families. Here are some of the tasks performed by a maid.

- Making of beds
- Washing dishes
- Laundry
- Cooking
- Ironing
- Running errors
- Babysitting

Etc. The list could go on and on. She is a gift from God.

Housekeeper

As a professional housekeeper, the main focus is to keep the value at the highest level in each home through maintenance cleaning. While we, too, are servants, and our goal is to keep the Client happy, our tasks are a little different. They include

- Dusting ceilings
- Window and track cleaning
- Woodwork cleaning
- Glass cleaning

Our list could go on and on as well, but the point I want to bring out is that our primary focus is the house and/or structure. The jobs we perform are a bit different, however modification is always possible.

Professional housekeeping is an art. It requires training, either by someone else or learning through trial and error. There was very little information out when we started in 1994, so trial and error was our teacher.

While learning on your own would be very time consuming and could take many years, this is the purpose for this book, to share with you the ins and outs of my twenty-five years' experience.

I have defined the professional Housekeeper, and I wish that were enough to convince you of your value to the world and the people in it. You are Very Important. Life is messy, no matter who you are or where you live. And it appears that everything we own has to be cleaned and/or maintained. So the information you will receive in this book will benefit you in all your cleaning needs, as a home-maker or as a professional.

While most of this information will also apply to the maid, our focus from here on out will be the Housekeeper and the residential home or business structure, occupied or empty.

Why are we so important? Let's take a look at some essential facts.

We give people what they need as well as what they want — a clean environment which allows more time for themselves so they can enjoy their lives.

Here are some important facts and benefits of maintaining a clean environment.

Cleaning Facts

Benefits to your health

Many allergies are caused by domestic dust and mold, according to some studies.

Regular cleanings in a residential home or structure provide more opportunities to detect mold growth and fix the problem promptly. Mold can cause all kinds of upper respiratory issues, even death in some cases. Mold and mildew are mentioned in the Bible as severe. Homes were burned down because of it.

Regular cleanings preserve your assets

Every two years, a well-known company called Home Gain surveys hundreds of Realtors, asking them what improvements they recommend for sellers.

Cleaning is recommended by 99% of Realtors as the number one thing a seller can do to increase the odds of selling quickly and at the best price. Many times this costs less than $300.00, but has a returning value of nearly $2,000 to the home's sale price, or a 586% return (ROI).

Self Esteem

Interestingly articles state a cluttered environment can cost you in energy, time and even money, whereas a clean, organized home can soothe you and provide a haven from stress, frees up time for fun with friends and family, and provides a place to feel safe and at peace.

TWO

Getting Started

A start-up of $300.00 will work.

- Licensing - $100.00 estimated
- Advertising – $100.00
- Supplies – $100.00 Rags, duster, mop, broom. Invest in a floor vacuum asap

Business cards and brochures will be helpful to have printed up, but a piece of paper with your name and phone number and the deal agreed upon will work until income is coming in.

- Unexpected cost – $200.00

Licensing

The information given here applies to the State in which you reside. You must gain knowledge of all the requirements for your State. No need to get frustrated or concerned at this point; it is an easy and straightforward process.

Regardless of the State, you will need to contact your State's business registration office either in person or online.

You will have several options. Below is an example.

<u>State Registration Office</u>

DBA / DOING BUSINESS AS/ FICTITIOUS NAME

If you are not going to use your name as the name of your company (example: John Smith), you're going to need a fictitious business name, or DBA (Doing Business As). With a DBA, you can legally publish your business name everywhere: the phone book, your business cards, advertisements, directories. You're putting yourself at risk without one.

This one is the best option to start with if funds are an issue.

LLC / LIMITED LIABILITY COMPANY

A limited liability company (LLC) has many advantages as a form of business entity.

CORP. / INC. / CORPORATION / INCOR-PORATION

There are many advantages to incorporating your business. Liability protection of your assets is one of the primary reasons why a small business will form a corporation. Incorporating helps to separate your assets from that of your business. A corporation is a legal entity that exists separately from its owners or shareholders.

You choose the one that meets your needs.

You can upgrade at any time.

While it is best to get this in place first, you can start by cleaning someone else's home, maybe yours or a family member's, to see if you want to commit. It is a commitment.

You will have a new boss for every job.

Before we start cleaning for others, we must understand the mindset of some housekeepers and the Clients.

Unfortunately, as a professional Housekeeper, not all people will see your worth in the beginning; this can be very discouraging. We still have those that want a housekeeper so that they do not have to clean anything. Not picking up after themselves, and even arranging for other jobs to be completed on the same day inside the home to get everything done in a day, not realizing this takes away from the quality of their cleaning. They do not understand. They need a maid, not a housekeeper. These conditions should not be acceptable for professional Housekeepers.

The Housekeeper who has never been in business for themselves must understand that the Clients are expecting them to perform a service for them on a regular basis, and you must respect their time and money. Show up on time and be consistent. Keep it business. While it is essential to get to know your clients on a business level so you can best meet their cleaning needs, mingling into their personal lives or bringing them into yours never works long term. You are there to serve them, not be their buddy. While I have many clients I enjoy spending time with, on cleaning day it's all about business. Many believe that being in business for themselves means they are their boss; while this is true in reality, every Client is a boss.

Cleaning is like any other job you perform. It requires focus. Each time you stop or get interrupted from your system, it takes time to get back on track. Some clients will think it needs to take all day to perform a specific task, not realizing there's a new and more efficient way to do the job now.

I have even had clients that open the window to air the house out while cleaning is going on. This makes no sense at all, letting dust and dirt inside while paying good money to remove it at the same time.

I say all this to say this: you need to know how to convince a client they need you to perform duties they either cannot or will not take care of, and you know what you are doing.

Living in a tourist town surrounded by motels, hotels, and condos gives an excellent opportunity for commercial work. With this proper understanding, the independent Housekeeper may take on these jobs as well.

Residential cleaning and condo/commercial cleaning are two very different ways of thinking and should be taken into consideration.

Residential cleaning is concentrated mainly on quality, where commercial is focused primarily on quantity. If it is a rental property, many, such as a motel, hotel, or condo, may have a tiny window to get the cleaning done before the new tenant arrives.

While quality must be the number one focus for residential cleaning, timing is essential as well. Once I have completed a job several times, staying with the same routine, I will start timing myself. I time every move right down to how many rags I use, to how many times you wipe something. You will be surprised how many times we clean an already clean surface. This is an excellent way to speed yourself up. I have even pretended I was training someone else. This keeps the mind not only focused on timing but quality too.

The time frame is essential for each job performed. Most homes will agree to a once a week, biweekly, or once every four weeks cleaning. Not once a month, but every four weeks. Some months have five weeks. But every four weeks.

Keep everything 100% clean. We can make adjustments to time and cost if needed.

THREE

Ideal Client

____

We also have what I like to call the perfect Client.

1. One or two people, adults of course, both have jobs/professions, so no one is home during the cleaning.

Although, there are some adults messier than children.

2. These people clean before you get there, so there's never a mess, and are very grateful for the help.

These people are hard to find, but they are out there. But how do we get them?

I will walk you through what I did from start to success.

Advertising

Once you have your license in place, you are now ready to let people know you are prepared to go to work.

I started with my local paper; running an ad for an entire month is less costly than just a few days, so I highly recommend running an ad for a thirty-day period in your local newspaper.

Free papers and websites are an excellent source for advertising. Craigslist, Facebook, friends, and family. Wherever you can get the word out.

You can later move on to the radio and TV advertising.

Business cards are a must. You can go with something simple like the name of your company with a phone number.

Flyers can be costly for someone with a small budget, but can be incorporated later.

▭

Handling calls can be challenging

It's always a good idea to practice what you are going to say ahead of time. Never give a price over the phone.

An accurate price can be determined best through an interview.

OK, now you get the call. What next?

Sample of a Business Call

Client – My name is Mrs. Carr. I am interested in your cleaning ad.

Me – Yes, this is Mary, thank you for calling. How can I help you?

Client – I need my home cleaned. How much do you charge per hour?

Me – What is the location of the property?

Client – I live in Lynn Haven.

Me – The job will be priced based on the type and amount

of work performed. An interview can determine an accurate price. There is no charge for the meeting, and you are under no obligation. Would you like to set up an appointment?

Client – Yes.

Me – Would Monday at 3:00 work for you?

Client – Yes.

If the answer is no, then maintain the control, never expecting them to control the conversation or the interview. They need to see our confidence. You can say something such as. I have 3:00 on Wednesday available would that be better.

Me – Could you please give me your physical address, your name and phone number in case it did not store in my phone?

Client – Kathy Carr, (654) 679-2367, 2234 East 18th Street, Lyn Havan.

Me – OK, we are all set. I will see you at 3:00 on Monday at 2234 East 18th Street in Lynn Haven. If anything changes, please give me a call. I will do the same. Thank you, and have a great day.

It is a good thing to be as professional as possible, but there will be times you will need just to lay all that aside and just let them tell you their whole life's story. And they will.

FOUR

The Interview
____

Always arrive on time, or a few minutes early, with a friendly smile and a warm greeting.

Listen for a minute and get an idea of what is needed. It is best just to listen and take note of the ultimate experience with the previous Housekeepers, if they share it.

It is best not to make them any promises outside your routine services offered to all. You might say something like, "I am sorry you have had a bad experience." Ask if you can take a look at the home/ business.

They will more than likely follow you around; this is OK.

I always start at the back of a structure and work my way to the front.

I will now walk you through a method I have learned over the years that has worked best for the Client and me.

I use this same pattern while performing the job as well, so please pay close attention. The Client will determine at this point if you know what you are doing or not.

Bedrooms

The first room more than likely will be a bedroom.

Since the ceiling fan is going to be the first thing cleaned, look there first. The dirtier the fan, the dirtier the entire house will be. If the A/C filter is full, dust will then begin to escape through the ductwork and vents, covering the whole house. If the fan has been in use, it will catch the dirt on the blades. It is recommended that an A/C filter be changed at least once a month in the summer when A/C is on. Every three months on heater months. Here is an excellent time to ask how long it has been since their last cleaning, and is there someone who changes the A/C filter on a regular basis. If you get the job, it is in your best interest to take on this task. Keeping it clean will be a big plus for you by cutting the dust down. It doesn't matter what the answer is. You are just gathering information useful to you.

Still in the same room, look at the pictures. The glass will have dried dust on them in some cases. Take your hand and run it across the glass. You are now identifying that all photographs and glass will reflect the same level of dirt. You are also telling them I know what I am doing.

Now you are at the furniture, still in the same room.

Pay close attention to the type of furniture they have. Is it wood, antique, raw wood, or painted? Look very closely at the grooves and patterns in the wood. A detailed cleaning will require a toothbrush to get inside the groves to remove dust. Identifying the type of wood will tell you what product to use and also help to determine how long it will take to clean each piece.

You will use this same pattern through the home, including living rooms, dining room and office.

Bathroom

Now you are in the bathroom.

Overhead light will be your first cleaning job in here. Removing and washing globes and cleaning bulbs as well.

Move your attention down to the sink. Do you see mildew? IF SO POINT IT OUT. Such as: "It looks like you are getting some mold starting to build up here." Note: if mildew is pink, it is alive and growing fast; if it is dark black, it has turned to mold and is growing quickly; it will cover the entire home, traveling through the A/C vents. The Client needs to know the danger of mold. It can cause death through upper respiratory problems. You will be using a toothbrush to clean around fixtures such as hot and cold water fixtures, toilet connectors, grout, and lining holders to remove any sign of mold/mildew. You will be cleaning all item on the sink, so be mindful of how much is there. You are determining time here as well as the level of dirt.

Tubs

What type of bathtub is it? Fiberglass, ceramic, or ceramic tile?

Is there any mildew? Your time could be double if mold and mildew are present. Adjust price accordingly. See tubs in the Appendix for instructions on cleaning at the back of the book.

Toilet

Toilets: how bad is it? How much mildew is hiding underneath? Get down or lean over so you can see the small holes under the rim. Mildew hides there. Let the Client see you look; this is detail cleaning.

Kitchen

Overhead lights/fans will be your starting point in this room.

Cabinets would be second. How bad are they? If wood, what type? How much grease buildup from hands and cooking is around the handles/knobs? Take note; this can be time-consuming.

Now you are at the counters. Starting from the back, then clean items last. Estimate how much time it will take. You will be cleaning small appliances, so check them too. Toaster, small ovens, microwaves, and coffee pots. Now to the stove. Never put an oven cleaner in the self-cleaning oven. However, some older appliances do not have self-cleaning; they will need to be cleaned manually, which could be very time-consuming. View cleaning ovens in the Appendix.

The refrigerator will need to be disassembled to get underneath the drawers on a detailed cleaning.

This generally takes about an hour and a half.

Laundry Room

Don't bypass this room. Washer and dryer will need to be cleaned/wiped down, then clean all areas including hot water heater.

After you have been in each room of the structure, the walkthrough, you now know what it will take to get the job done well.

As you are looking at the home/business, it is vital that you remain focused on the interview and not get into a personal conversation at this point. That can come after the meeting.

After you have gone through the entire home, ask the Client if it would be OK for you to walk through one more time alone, to calculate your time. This will help you focus and give you the ability to provide accurate timing and price for performing the job.

<hr>

Hopefully, you have made some good notes. Now it's time to make a decision: how much to charge. Have in your mind a minimized price that goes with any job. It can be $50.00 or $100.00, whatever your market will bear. My process is to think about what I believe it's worth, and I go $25.00 below that. If I don't get the job, I will be OK knowing I offered a deal.

What if you don't have a clue? Start with your minimized price. You will grow in this area over time and gain the confidence you need to deliver with ease and confidence.

Present Price to the Client.

So now you have an excellent idea how long it will take to do a good job and that you and the Client will be proud. Now how much do we charge per hour? While we don't work hourly, knowing how much you would like to make per hour will help get to a price.

Ten hours of work at $100.00 is ten dollars an hour. Give them three prices, a detail cleaning price, meaning you clean everything all at one time. This price is usually twice as much as the basic clean.

Then the basic cleaning price, both weekly and biweekly. This is to maintain detail cleaning. Basic cleaning consists of dusting all areas with a duster, cleaning bathroom, kitchen, and floors. The basic cleaning requires less time, therefore, you can charge less.

Example

Detail cleaning $300.00

Basic cleaning $125.00 per week

Biweekly $150.00

Monthly. $200.00 (every four weeks).

You can reply by saying something such as: "OK, I think I have come up with a price." At this point, you can point out some negative and positive aspects.

Example: I think I have got you a price. I want to say that you have done a great job keeping up with the cleaning.

Example: Due to the mildew and/or dust level, the price will be this — Give them the prices in the order above, starting with the detail, then weekly price, lastly the biweekly price. Pause between each price and let them think because they don't know what they need at this point. Let them choose. Let them know they can upgrade at any time.

Set a Cleaning Date Right Then

Me: I have Tuesday available to start, would that work for you?

Always let them supply the cleaning products and a carpet vacuum. You provide clothes, duster, brushes, floor vacuum, and mop.

If the Client has seen you do a great job on the walk-through, at this point, they will either take it or tell you they want to allow someone else to look, and they will give you a call later. At this point, you must move on. It has been my experience, the shorter the interview, the better.

Again I must say avoid personal involvement/ conversations at this point. Keep it business.

Once an agreement is in place, avoid all changes on your part regarding the time. Show up early with a great attitude and do a great job. You are on your way to success.

It is good to practice this at home. Take a note pad and do an interview of your own house. Before long you will be doing this everywhere you go.

Who is the Housekeeper?

Anyone who wants to earn from $10,000 to $100,000 can benefit from this industry. The sky's the limit.

I am convinced that anyone can benefit from this profession. If you live in a tourist town and are not taking advantage of this easy to run business, you are missing out. You learn, then you train others. It's that simple. If you are retired, this is a great way to bring in extra income, and you can choose how much you want to work. The steps to getting started are easy and quick. Let's go over the steps again just to make sure they are clear.

Step 1

Read this book, then clean a house to see what it's like following these instructions. After reading this book, you now know what you are doing.

Start with your own. Walk through, monitor your time, and clean it. Do this more than once.

I would like to say this is what I did, but that's not true. I thought my house was clean. LOL

I had a small child at the time, and cleaning my house seemed useless. Then I went to someone's home, and it was spotless, and she had three children. Funny how that works, but I have often heard that when the student is ready, the teacher will appear, and this is so true. I also had a lady ask me If she could come to see my house before I looked at hers. What? What a wakeup call for me. I decided that day that my home would be and stay the cleanest house I cleaned. Which was not easy, for I had many habits I had to break, like making sure my shoes went in the closet when I removed them, and not left in the living room or wherever I took them off. This took about a month to change, but a funny thing happened: I stopped picking up other people's shoes too. It was almost as though they knew better than even to think I would stoop down and pick them up. I can't explain how that worked, but it did.

Step 2

Now get your licenses to do business.

I started with a DBA (Doing Business As). Cleaning in Detail by Barbara, this was the name of my company. My Tax ID was my social security number. I purchased a calendar, which I took to my tax person at the end of the year. Each day I wrote down the name of the person I cleaned for that day and how much money I made for that day. If more than one house, they both went down on that day. I would then total it up at the end of the week and later the month. Easy bookkeeping. Please don't make the mistake of renting an office or buying a car or even purchasing anything you don't need to perform the job. I did all that because It made me feel important; did nothing to bring in clients.

Step 3

Advertise your business.

As I have already said, I started with my local paper. Cleaning in Detail by Barbara was my ad with my phone number. It helps to be licensed, bonded, and insured, but bonding and insurance can come later. If you can start at the top with all that, by all means, do so.

Step 4

Answer the call. I ran the ad and was afraid to answer the phone. Some people will simply not leave a message or return the call, so answer the call. You can have a friend call you for practice. LOL. Set up the interview.

Step 5

Do the interview. Show up on time. Not early and not late. The people are getting ready for you too. If they start telling you about how bad off their life is and how they need you to go as cheap as possible, think nothing of it, do not let this sway you from your process. I have done this as well. I had a lady that acted like she was crazy yelling at her husband, who had called me to get me out of her house. Poor man needed help. I went below my pricing. When I left the house the whole street was named after her. They could afford it, but remember everybody is looking for a deal, including us. I am not saying don't be compassionate with people. Follow your heart on that one. You are in business for yourself, and you can do whatever you like. I have even done jobs for free. The good deed always comes back with rewards. My experience is, if they have a problem with the price, it is best to walk away. Most times if you go down on your cost, you have lost their confidence in what you are doing. This hurts, but the hurt will build your confidence in yourself and your position. If you don't get the job, don't worry, they call back in many cases.

Step 6

Do the job, and do it well. Follow the pattern in cleaning the house.

Make sure you have their next cleaning already on your calendar.

Step 7

Collect your check with a smile, even if it took you longer than you thought, also if you didn't make as much as you would have liked. This is the hard part of learning business. Treat each Client with respect.

Use this book as a guide for cleaning and refer to the Appendix as often as needed and happy cleaning.

FIVE

Cleaning the House

AN EASY SIMPLE AND EASY PROCESS TO CLEANING A
HOUSE.

This sounds a little silly; you would think we would clean our own home just like anyone else's home. Something weird happens when we do our own house, we throw in all these other tasks.

Laundry, cooking, listening to the radio, watching TV, and redecorating/rearranging everything in the house. We end up working all day and not accomplishing our goal, which was to clean the house and get it done so we can enjoy the rest of our day. Right? Well, as I have stated earlier in the book, cleaning requires focus. This seems to be hard at our house because we have the freedom to work at our own pace. Nothing wrong with this, but assuming you want to get the job done in a timely manner, we need focus. I will now lead you through it as an easy and simple process. This process or pattern can be used to clean any house.

Cleaning your own home

We need to decide how deep we will go in a day. Split up the detail cleaning. By this I mean one day just do the deep exterior cleaning. This is everything that is visible in a walkthrough. Inside the refrigerator, stoves, closets, save these for another day. Before any cleaning can be done, we must gain access to all areas of the house. By this, I mean pick up and put away everything that is out of place. Books, mail, shoes, clothes, everything that does not belongs were it is right now. You may need to get rid of a few things. If this is the case, while deciding, instead of looking for what to get rid of, look for what you need to keep. This works much better. Every item should have a home or a designated place. Shoes belong in the closet, dishes belong in a cabinet. This may take a while, but put everything away before you clean.

Now that we have this completed, let's jump right into cleaning. Start at the back of the house, possibly a bedroom or a bathroom. I will walk you through a very simple process. You will need toilet bowl cleaner, maybe some Murphy's Oil Soap for wood and Clorox Clean-Up. Be very careful with any product that has Clorox, it can stain your clothes. And we will need a toothbrush. You will need some small rags for cleaning and some medium ones for drying; terrycloth seems to work best. We will start with a bathroom.

Bathroom

First put in the toilet bowl cleaner. Next, spray the toilet seat and tub/shower with the Clorox Clean-Up so every-thing can be loosening up while you start with the mirror. Spray extra cleaner on any mildew areas, black and/or pink.

Don't spray the sink just yet.

Mirrors

Take a small, clean cloth and wet it with water and wipe the entire mirror, even if it looks clean. Wipe until all areas seem smooth to the hand. Hairspray, powder, and even lint from toilet paper can build up on the mirror. Now begin drying with the larger rag. Wipe in a pattern either up and down or across. Keep this pattern until the mirror is smooth and completely dry. You will see lint while drying, but it will simply fall off once it's dry. Many cleaning products for glass have wax in them and a drying agent that causes it to dry too fast, leaving smears behind. Water will not do this. Just make sure you are continually wiping until it's dry. Clean all mirrors and glass in the room at one time.

Sink

Now you can pull everything forward away from the back. Put everything inside the sink to get more room if needed. Spray the back with Clorox Clean-Up, then wipe and dry. Before you put anything back in place, make sure you have cleaned it first. You can now spray the entire sink down, paying close attention to the hot and cold knobs and faucet. Mildew likes to build up here. Taking your toothbrush clean around those and any hard to get areas. Clean the rest and dry. You can save the outside cabinets for another day. You could even pick one day and do woodwork only. Doors, baseboards, and cabinets.

Toilets

Now that is has already been sprayed, take your toilet bowl brush and clean the inside, paying close attention to those little holes underneath the bowl. This is where mildew builds up. Take your brush and force it into the bottom hole. This will loosen any mildew. With the toothbrush, go around all attachments, seat, and the base screws. If you have boys in the house, you may need to use the brush around the base as well to remove any urine stains. Now clean the entire outside bowl, including the base, then dry.

Tub/Shower

Everything should be loosened up by now; start with wetting the shower/tub, getting your rag good and wet. Now go up the sides, wiping all areas again. You may need to brush any dark spots. Work your way down to the sides of the tub/shower. Do the bottom last. All areas should feel smooth to the hand; if not, you still have soap scum. Clean a little longer, or you may need a little more cleaner.

Now the bathroom is complete except the floor. Vacuum first, then mop with vinegar and water.

All done.

Bedroom

Now we are in the bedroom. Always dust everything in the room first with a duster to remove all loose dust. Take a clean rag and wet lightly with water and clean the mirrors first, using the same pattern you did in the bathroom. Take that same rag and clean everything else in the room other than wood; no cleaner is needed for this. This includes lamps, bulbs, pictures, etc. Now take a rag and, in a sink or bucket, mix up some water and Murphy's Oil Soap. Wash all wood, including fans. You can leave the doors and baseboards for another day.

Use this same pattern for cleaning all other rooms in the home except the kitchen and laundry room. Dust first, next clean the glass, then the wood. If the floor is really bad, vacuum first. This will prevent dust from rising. Proceed with dusting. Note: if you are using a broom, sweep in every room first.

I highly recommend that you invest in a good floor

vacuum, this will save you lots of time. It is a must if you are in business.

Kitchen

We will start by dusting everything, including the fan first, and then the counters. Move everything forward on the counters, spray behind items and let it sit to loosen any dirt. While you are waiting, get your Murphy's Oil Soap rag and clean the fan. I recommend doing the face of all cabinets in this room. You may have splatters and oil from your hands,= that has built up over time. Now go back to the counters and clean first and then dry, making sure to clean all items before placing them back in place. This also includes all small appliances. Toasters, ovens, can openers, blenders, etc. Now do your floors.

You're done, another job completed. One more room to go. This is a very simple process; stay focused on what you are doing; if the phone rings, let it go until you finish what you are doing. Remember, every time you stop, it will take time to get back on track.

Laundry Room

This room gets very dusty, and you may need to use the vacuum with attachments here. After removing all dust, now you are ready to start cleaning. Using your Clorox rag, wipe down all appliances, including the hot water heater, if it is located in the laundry room. Lift the lid on the washer, spray cleaner around door attachments, and use the toothbrush to remove all buildup. Don't forget the soap dispenser. That will need cleaning as well. If you have a front load washer, you will need to pull out the soap compartment and clean with a toothbrush; mildew can build up anywhere water is allowed to sit. On the dryer, the toothbrush can remove most dirt around the door attachments easily. We will also need to clean the lint trap and, of course, the floor. Now stand back and see if you have missed anything; if not, you're all done.

Now, after we clean up, we are now ready to enjoy the rest of our day, and we can end it relaxing in a nice, clean environment. Be proud of yourself, you did a great job.

About the Author

Barbara is not just a Housekeeper. She is a sought out author, teacher, motivator, certified speaker, workshop facilitator, and leader. Founder of The Process to Victory and Author of The Process by Barbara Nethery, which leads us throughs a Spiritual house cleaning. Life gets messy, and we pick up a lot of unhealthy attitudes, mindsets, and resentments along the way. Barbara also conducts workshops to help her audience work through the easy steps in her book. She has touched the lives of many with her unique style of teaching that not only lights up the room but creates an atmosphere of love and safety; as a result people's hearts open up, they are set free.
She resides in Panama City Beach, FL.

Appendix

Most cleaning products today contain some form of wax, which can create a buildup over time

while you may have a shine for a very short period, this can ruin your furniture.

I believe it is best to use natural products, unscented; this is important when cleaning for others. Many people have allergies to some products. It is a good idea to mention this to a client if you have any health issues. Many products require rinsing after cleaning. It is a good thing to always go by the manufactory's instructions.

A

A/C

This is the area where the A/C filter sits. Use the vacuum to remove dust on all areas on the unit, wipe with water, use cleaner for tough stains. If you have rust, you can use a Brillo pad if needed.

Permanent A/C Filters

Brush or vacuum off loose dust and then wash with water. It is best to have water with pressure to push out the dirt.

A/C Vents

Dust, brush or vacuum off loose dust first, then apply cleaner and brush to cleanliness.

B

Baskets

Use a vacuum with the brush to remove loose dust; the item can then be sprayed with pressured water to remove dirt. No cleaner needed.

Books

Dust or vacuum to free dirt. No cleaner needed

C

Cabinets

For natural wood, you will need a wood soap or wood cleaner to wash the entire surface. Then you can apply wax to condition the wood. All additional cleans should only require a damp cloth to remove stains. Regular waxing will create a buildup at some point; this can and does dry out the wood. So every three months is an excellent time frame on waxing.

Painted wood

Water is all you will need to remove dirt. A small amount of vinegar will remove most stains. A cleaner can be applied if needed. Never spray the product directly on surface, some area will be bleached while others won't, leaving bleached streaks.

Curtains

Vacuum or use a clean, dry brush. No spot cleaning can efficiently work.

Cabinets

If wood, use instructions for wood. If granite, do not use any products that are not specified for granite.

D

Dryer

Clorox and water

Doors

See wood instruction on wood. If metal, use Clorox Clean-Up on a rag only.

E

F

Fans

Clean all light globes and bulbs. Clean fan blades with water.

Floors

Ceramic tile – vinegar and water. For wood, use wood instructions. For vinyl, use vinegar and water.

Hardwood – Use oil soap, then rinse, or just plain water.

Vinyl Floors – If someone has put wax on the vinyl floors, use ammonia and water to remove wax, then clean with vinegar and water to remove and film. Waxing may be applied after cleaning. Wax every three months thereafter.

Laminated floors – Clean with a small amount of vinegar and water.

Marble – Use water or marble cleaner only. Never use ammonia or vinegar and water, this can damage marble by removing the finish.

G

Glass

Use ammonia and water or vinegar and water. You can also use plain water. I stay away from all glass cleaner.

Globes

Clean with vinegar and water or just plain water.

H

I

J

K

L

Lamps

Clean with water.

Light bulbs

Clean with water only.

M

Metal

clean and shine with WD-40 or with metal cleaner.

Microwaves

Clorox cleaner, or vinegar and water.

Mildew

Use Clorox and water and a brush.

N

O

P

Pictures

Clean with vinegar and water or just water.

Plants

Use a duster or vacuum only.

Q

R

Refrigerators

Clean with vinegar and water.

S

Stoves

Always use self-cleaning if you have the option. If not, use a basic oven cleaner plus SOS pad if needed. You can also use a razor, being careful not to scratch surface.

Sinks

Use Clorox cleaner and water. If they are marbled, use marble cleaner only or plain water.

Shades

Vacuum or dust; do not wet.

T

Toilet

Toilet bowl cleaner and a good toilet brush. Clorox can be used if you have tough stains.

Tubs

Scrubbing Bubbles works best for me. Clorox cleaner works great, as well.

U

V

Vents

Clorox Clean-Up, a brush, and a rag for cleaning, then dry.

W

Windows

Vinegar and water. Ammonia and water for tough stains.

Washer

Clorox cleaner for outside only.

Wood

Plain/Natural Wood – water only

Painted wood – Clorox and water or just plain water.

Stained – water only, no scrubbing.

X

Y

Z

Afterword

It has been my pleasure to share my experience with you. Please keep it simple, and always do your very best.

Happy Cleaning.